THIS WEDDING PLANNER
BELONGS TO:

WEDDING DETAILS

WEDDING DATE & TIME:

TO DO LIST:

VENUE ADDRESS:

BUDGET:

OFFICIANT:

WEDDING PARTY:

NOTES & REMINDERS:

WEDDING BUDGET

	TOTAL COST:	DEPOSIT:	REMAINDER:
WEDDING VENUE			
RECEPTION VENUE			
FLORIST			
OFFICIANT			
CATERER			
WEDDING CAKE			
BRIDAL ATTIRE			
GROOM ATTIRE			
BRIDAL JEWELRY			
BRIDESMAID ATTIRE			
GROOMSMEN ATTIRE			
HAIR & MAKE UP			
PHOTOGRAPHER			
VIDEOGRAPHER			
DJ SERVICE/ENTERTAINMENT			
INVITATIONS			
TRANSPORTATION			
WEDDING PARTY GIFTS			
RENTALS			
HONEYMOON			

12 MONTHS BEFORE

SET THE DATE

SET YOUR BUDGET

CHOOSE YOUR THEME

ORGANIZE ENGAGEMENT PARTY

RESEARCH VENUES

BOOK A WEDDING PLANNER

RESEARCH PHOTOGRAPHERS

RESEARCH VIDEOGRAPHERS

RESEARCH DJ'S/ENTERTAINMENT

CONSIDER FLORISTS

RESEARCH CATERERS

DECIDE ON OFFICIANT

CREATE INITIAL GUEST LIST

CHOOSE WEDDING PARTY

SHOP FOR WEDDING DRESS

REGISTER WITH GIFT REGISTRY

DISCUSS HONEYMOON IDEAS

RESEARCH WEDDING RINGS

THINGS TO REMEMBER:

9 MONTHS BEFORE

FINALIZE GUEST LIST

ORDER INVITATIONS

PLAN YOUR RECEPTION

BOOK PHOTOGRAPHER

BOOK VIDEOGRAPHER

BOOK FLORIST

BOOK DJ/ENTERTAINMENT

BOOK CATERER

CHOOSE WEDDING CAKE

CHOOSE WEDDING GOWN

ORDER BRIDESMAIDS DRESSES

RESERVE TUXEDOS

ARRANGE TRANSPORTATION

BOOK WEDDING VENUE

BOOK RECEPTION VENUE

PLAN HONEYMOON

BOOK OFFICIANT

BOOK ROOMS FOR GUESTS

THINGS TO REMEMBER:

6 MONTHS BEFORE

ORDER THANK YOU NOTES

REVIEW RECEPTION DETAILS

MAKE APPT FOR DRESS FITTING

CONFIRM BRIDEMAIDS DRESSES

GET MARRIAGE LICENSE

BOOK HAIR/MAKE UP STYLIST

CONFIRM MUSIC SELECTIONS

PLAN BRIDAL SHOWER

PLAN REHEARSAL

SHOP FOR WEDDING RINGS

THINGS TO REMEMBER:

3 MONTHS BEFORE

MAIL OUT INVITATIONS

MEET WITH OFFICIANT

BUY GIFTS FOR WEDDING PARTY

BOOK FINAL GOWN FITTING

BUY WEDDING BANDS

PLAN YOUR HAIR STYLE

PURCHASE SHOES/HEELS

CONFIRM PASSPORTS ARE VALID

FINALIZE RECEPTION MENU

PLAN REHEARSAL DINNER

CONFIRM ALL BOOKINGS

APPLY FOR MARRIAGE LICENSE

CONFIRM MUSIC SELECTIONS

DRAFT WEDDING VOWS

CHOOSE YOUR MC

ARRANGE AIRPORT TRANSFER

THINGS TO REMEMBER:

1 MONTH BEFORE

CONFIRM FINAL GUEST COUNT

CONFIRM RECEPTION DETAILS

ATTEND FINAL GOWN FITTING

CONFIRM PHOTOGRAPHER

WRAP WEDDING PARTY GIFTS

CREATE PHOTOGRAPHY SHOT LIST

REHEARSE WEDDING VOWS

BOOK MANI-PEDI

CONFIRM WITH FLORIST

CONFIRM VIDEOGRAPHER

PICK UP BRIDEMAIDS DRESSES

CREATE WEDDING SCHEDULE

THINGS TO REMEMBER:

1 WEEK BEFORE

FINALIZE SEATING PLANS

MAKE PAYMENTS TO VENDORS

PACK FOR HONEYMOON

CONFIRM HOTEL RESERVATIONS

GIVE SCHEDULE TO PARTY

DELIVER LICENSE TO OFFICIANT

CONFIRM WITH BAKERY

PICK UP WEDDING DRESS

PICK UP TUXEDOS

GIVE MUSIC LIST TO DJ

THINGS TO REMEMBER:

1 DAY BEFORE

GET MANICURE/PEDICURE

ATTEND REHEARSAL DINNER

GET A GOOD NIGHT'S SLEEP!

GIVE GIFTS TO WEDDING PARTY

FINALIZE PACKING

TO DO LIST:

THE BIG DAY!

GET HAIR & MAKE UP DONE

HAVE A HEALTHY BREAKFAST

ENJOY YOUR BIG DAY!

MEET WITH BRIDESMAIDS

GIVE RINGS TO BEST MAN

TO DO LIST:

EVENTS

ENGAGEMENT PARTY:

DATE:

LOCATION:

TIME:

NUMBER OF GUESTS:

NOTES:

BRIDAL SHOWER:

DATE:

LOCATION:

TIME:

NUMBER OF GUESTS:

NOTES:

STAG & DOE PARTY:

DATE:

LOCATION:

TIME:

NUMBER OF GUESTS:

NOTES:

BRIDAL PARTY - THE LADIES

MAID OF HONOR:

PHONE: DRESS SIZE: SHOE SIZE:

EMAIL:

MATRON OF HONOR:

PHONE: DRESS SIZE: SHOE SIZE:

EMAIL:

BRIDESMAID #1:

PHONE: DRESS SIZE: SHOE SIZE:

EMAIL:

BRIDESMAID #2:

PHONE: DRESS SIZE: SHOE SIZE:

EMAIL:

BRIDESMAID #3:

PHONE: DRESS SIZE: SHOE SIZE:

EMAIL:

BRIDESMAID #4:

PHONE: DRESS SIZE: SHOE SIZE:

EMAIL:

NOTES:

BRIDAL PARTY - THE LADIES

MOTHER OF THE BRIDE:

PHONE: DRESS SIZE: SHOE SIZE:

EMAIL:

MOTHER OF THE GROOM:

PHONE: DRESS SIZE: SHOE SIZE:

EMAIL:

BRIDESMAID #5:

PHONE: DRESS SIZE: SHOE SIZE:

EMAIL:

BRIDESMAID #6:

PHONE: DRESS SIZE: SHOE SIZE:

EMAIL:

BRIDESMAID #7:

PHONE: DRESS SIZE: SHOE SIZE:

EMAIL:

BRIDESMAID #8:

PHONE: DRESS SIZE: SHOE SIZE:

EMAIL:

NOTES:

BRIDAL PARTY – THE GENTLEMEN

BEST MAN:

PHONE: WAIST SIZE: SHOE SIZE:

NECK SIZE: SLEEVE SIZE: JACKET SIZE:

EMAIL:

GROOMSMEN #1:

PHONE: WAIST SIZE: SHOE SIZE:

NECK SIZE: SLEEVE SIZE: JACKET SIZE:

EMAIL:

GROOMSMEN #2:

PHONE: WAIST SIZE: SHOE SIZE:

NECK SIZE: SLEEVE SIZE: JACKET SIZE:

EMAIL:

GROOMSMEN #3:

PHONE: WAIST SIZE: SHOE SIZE:

NECK SIZE: SLEEVE SIZE: JACKET SIZE:

EMAIL:

GROOMSMEN #4:

PHONE: WAIST SIZE: SHOE SIZE:

NECK SIZE: SLEEVE SIZE: JACKET SIZE:

EMAIL:

NOTES:

BRIDAL PARTY – THE GENTLEMEN

FATHER OF THE GROOM:

PHONE: WAIST SIZE: SHOE SIZE:

NECK SIZE: SLEEVE SIZE: JACKET SIZE:

EMAIL:

FATHER OF THE BRIDE:

PHONE: WAIST SIZE: SHOE SIZE:

NECK SIZE: SLEEVE SIZE: JACKET SIZE:

EMAIL:

GROOMSMEN #5:

PHONE: WAIST SIZE: SHOE SIZE:

NECK SIZE: SLEEVE SIZE: JACKET SIZE:

EMAIL:

GROOMSMEN #6:

PHONE: WAIST SIZE: SHOE SIZE:

NECK SIZE: SLEEVE SIZE: JACKET SIZE:

EMAIL:

GROOMSMEN #7:

PHONE: WAIST SIZE: SHOE SIZE:

NECK SIZE: SLEEVE SIZE: JACKET SIZE:

EMAIL:

GROOMSMEN #8:

PHONE: WAIST SIZE: SHOE SIZE:

NECK SIZE: SLEEVE SIZE: JACKET SIZE:

EMAIL:

PHOTOGRAPHER

PHOTOGRAPHER:

PHONE: **COMPANY:**

EMAIL: **ADDRESS:**

WEDDING PACKAGE OVERVIEW:

EST PRICE:

INCLUSIONS: YES ✓   NO ✓ COST:

ENGAGEMENT SHOOT:

PHOTO ALBUMS:

FRAMES:

PROOFS INCLUDED:

NEGATIVES INCLUDED:

TOTAL COST:

VIDEOGRAPHER

VIDEOGRAPHER:

PHONE: COMPANY:

EMAIL: ADDRESS:

WEDDING PACKAGE OVERVIEW:

EST PRICE:

INCLUSIONS: YES ✓   NO ✓   COST:

DUPLICATES/COPIES:

PHOTO MONTAGE:

MUSIC ADDED:

EDITING:

TOTAL COST:

NOTES:

DJ/ENTERTAINMENT

DJ/LIVE BAND/ENTERTAINMENT:

PHONE: COMPANY:

EMAIL: ADDRESS:

START TIME: END TIME:

ENTERTAINMENT SERVICE OVERVIEW:

EST PRICE:

INCLUSIONS: YES ✓   NO ✓   COST:

SOUND EQUIPMENT:

LIGHTING:

SPECIAL EFFECTS:

GRATUITIES

TOTAL COST:

NOTES:

FLORIST

FLORIST:

PHONE: COMPANY:

EMAIL: ADDRESS:

FLORAL PACKAGE:

EST PRICE: _____

INCLUSIONS: YES ✓   NO ✓   COST:

BRIDAL BOUQUET:

THROW AWAY BOUQUET:

CORSAGES:

CEREMONY FLOWERS

CENTERPIECES

CAKE TOPPER

BOUTONNIERE

TOTAL COST:

WEDDING CAKE/BAKER

PHONE: COMPANY:

EMAIL: ADDRESS:

WEDDING CAKE PACKAGE:

COST: _____   FREE TASTING: _____   DELIVERY FEE: _____

FLAVOR:

FILLING:

SIZE:

SHAPE:

COLOR:

EXTRAS:

TOTAL COST:

NOTES:

TRANSPORTATION

TO CEREMONY: PICK UP TIME: PICK UP LOCATION:

BRIDE:

GROOM:

BRIDE'S PARENTS:

GROOM'S PARENTS:

BRIDESMAIDS:

GROOMSMEN:

NOTES:

TO RECEPTION: PICK UP TIME: PICK UP LOCATION:

BRIDE & GROOM:

BRIDE'S PARENTS:

GROOM'S PARENTS:

BRIDESMAIDS:

GROOMSMEN:

MORE EVENTS

BACHELORETTE PARTY:

DATE:

LOCATION:

TIME:

NUMBER OF GUESTS:

NOTES:

BACHELOR PARTY:

DATE:

LOCATION:

TIME:

NUMBER OF GUESTS:

NOTES:

CEREMONY REHEARSAL:

DATE:

LOCATION:

TIME:

NUMBER OF GUESTS:

NOTES:

MORE EVENTS

REHEARSAL DINNER:

DATE: LOCATION:

TIME: NUMBER OF GUESTS:

   NOTES:

RECEPTION:

DATE: LOCATION:

TIME: NUMBER OF GUESTS:

   NOTES:

   REMINDERS:

CONTACTS

CEREMONY:

PHONE:

CONTACT NAME:

EMAIL:

ADDRESS:

RECEPTION:

PHONE:

CONTACT NAME:

EMAIL:

ADDRESS:

OFFICIANT:

PHONE:

CONTACT NAME:

EMAIL:

ADDRESS:

WEDDING PLANNER:

PHONE:

CONTACT NAME:

EMAIL:

ADDRESS:

CATERER:

PHONE:

CONTACT NAME:

EMAIL:

ADDRESS:

FLORIST:

PHONE:

CONTACT NAME:

EMAIL:

ADDRESS:

CONTACTS

BAKERY:

PHONE:

CONTACT NAME:

EMAIL:

ADDRESS:

BRIDAL SHOP:

PHONE:

CONTACT NAME:

EMAIL:

ADDRESS:

PHOTOGRAPHER:

PHONE:

CONTACT NAME:

EMAIL:

ADDRESS:

VIDEOGRAPHER:

PHONE:

CONTACT NAME:

EMAIL:

ADDRESS:

DJ/ENTERTAINMENT:

PHONE:

CONTACT NAME:

EMAIL:

ADDRESS:

HAIR/NAIL SALON:

PHONE:

CONTACT NAME:

EMAIL:

ADDRESS:

CONTACTS

MAKE UP ARTIST:

PHONE:

CONTACT NAME:

EMAIL:

ADDRESS:

RENTALS:

PHONE:

CONTACT NAME:

EMAIL:

ADDRESS:

HONEYMOON RESORT/HOTEL:

PHONE:

CONTACT NAME:

EMAIL:

ADDRESS:

TRANSPORTATION SERVICE:

PHONE:

CONTACT NAME:

EMAIL:

ADDRESS:

NOTES:

CATERER DETAILS

CONTACT INFORMATION:

PHONE:

CONTACT NAME:

EMAIL:

ADDRESS:

MENU CHOICE #1:

MENU CHOICE #2:

YES ✓　　NO ✓　　COST:

BAR INCLUDED:

CORKAGE FEE:

HORS D'OEUVRES:

TAXES INCLUDED:

GRATUITIES INCLUDED:

MENU

HORS D'OEUVRES

1st COURSE:

2nd COURSE:

3rd COURSE:

4th COURSE:

DESSERT:

1 WEEK BEFORE

THINGS TO DO: NOTES:

MONDAY

TUESDAY

WEDNESDAY

THURSDAY

REMINDERS & NOTES:

1 WEEK BEFORE

THINGS TO DO:

NOTES:

FRIDAY

SATURDAY

SUNDAY

LEFT TO DO:

REMINDERS:

NOTES:

WEDDING GUEST LIST

NAME:	ADDRESS:	# IN PARTY:	RSVP: ✓

WEDDING GUEST LIST

NAME:	ADDRESS:	# IN PARTY:	RSVP: ✓

WEDDING GUEST LIST

NAME:	ADDRESS:	# IN PARTY:	RSVP: ✓

WEDDING GUEST LIST

NAME:	ADDRESS:	# IN PARTY:	RSVP: ✓

WEDDING GUEST LIST

NAME:	ADDRESS:	# IN PARTY:	RSVP: ✓

WEDDING GUEST LIST

NAME:	ADDRESS:	# IN PARTY:	RSVP: ✓

WEDDING GUEST LIST

NAME:	ADDRESS:	# IN PARTY:	RSVP: ✓

WEDDING GUEST LIST

NAME:	ADDRESS:	# IN PARTY:	RSVP: ✓

WEDDING GUEST LIST

NAME:	ADDRESS:	# IN PARTY:	RSVP: ✓

WEDDING GUEST LIST

NAME:	ADDRESS:	# IN PARTY:	RSVP: ✓

WEDDING GUEST LIST

NAME:	ADDRESS:	# IN PARTY:	RSVP: ✓

WEDDING GUEST LIST

NAME:	ADDRESS:	# IN PARTY:	RSVP: ✓

WEDDING GUEST LIST

NAME:	ADDRESS:	# IN PARTY:	RSVP: ✓

WEDDING GUEST LIST

NAME:	ADDRESS:	# IN PARTY:	RSVP: ✓

WEDDING GUEST LIST

NAME:	ADDRESS:	# IN PARTY:	RSVP: ✓

WEDDING GUEST LIST

NAME:	ADDRESS:	# IN PARTY:	RSVP: ✓

WEDDING GUEST LIST

NAME:	ADDRESS:	# IN PARTY:	RSVP: ✓

WEDDING GUEST LIST

NAME:	ADDRESS:	# IN PARTY:	RSVP: ✓

WEDDING GUEST LIST

NAME:	ADDRESS:	# IN PARTY:	RSVP: ✓

WEDDING GUEST LIST

NAME:	ADDRESS:	# IN PARTY:	RSVP: ✓

WEDDING GUEST LIST

NAME:	ADDRESS:	# IN PARTY:	RSVP: ✓

WEDDING GUEST LIST

NAME:	ADDRESS:	# IN PARTY:	RSVP: ✓

WEDDING GUEST LIST

NAME:	ADDRESS:	# IN PARTY:	RSVP: ✓

WEDDING GUEST LIST

NAME:	ADDRESS:	# IN PARTY:	RSVP: ✓

WEDDING GUEST LIST

NAME:	ADDRESS:	# IN PARTY:	RSVP: ✓

WEDDING GUEST LIST

NAME:	ADDRESS:	# IN PARTY:	RSVP: ✓

WEDDING GUEST LIST

NAME:	ADDRESS:	# IN PARTY:	RSVP: ✓

WEDDING GUEST LIST

NAME:	ADDRESS:	# IN PARTY:	RSVP: ✓

WEDDING GUEST LIST

NAME:	ADDRESS:	# IN PARTY:	RSVP: ✓

WEDDING GUEST LIST

NAME:	ADDRESS:	# IN PARTY:	RSVP: ✓

WEDDING GUEST LIST

NAME:	ADDRESS:	# IN PARTY:	RSVP: ✓

WEDDING GUEST LIST

NAME:	ADDRESS:	# IN PARTY:	RSVP: ✓

WEDDING GUEST LIST

NAME:	ADDRESS:	# IN PARTY:	RSVP: ✓

WEDDING GUEST LIST

NAME:	ADDRESS:	# IN PARTY:	RSVP: ✓

WEDDING GUEST LIST

NAME:	ADDRESS:	# IN PARTY:	RSVP: ✓

WEDDING GUEST LIST

NAME:	ADDRESS:	# IN PARTY:	RSVP: ✓

WEDDING GUEST LIST

NAME:	ADDRESS:	# IN PARTY:	RSVP: ✓

WEDDING GUEST LIST

NAME:	ADDRESS:	# IN PARTY:	RSVP: ✓

WEDDING GUEST LIST

NAME:	ADDRESS:	# IN PARTY:	RSVP: ✓

WEDDING GUEST LIST

NAME:	ADDRESS:	# IN PARTY:	RSVP: ✓

WEDDING GUEST LIST

NAME:	ADDRESS:	# IN PARTY:	RSVP: ✓

WEDDING GUEST LIST

NAME:	ADDRESS:	# IN PARTY:	RSVP: ✓

WEDDING GUEST LIST

NAME:	ADDRESS:	# IN PARTY:	RSVP: ✓

WEDDING GUEST LIST

NAME:	ADDRESS:	# IN PARTY:	RSVP: ✓

WEDDING GUEST LIST

NAME:	ADDRESS:	# IN PARTY:	RSVP: ✓

WEDDING GUEST LIST

NAME:	ADDRESS:	# IN PARTY:	RSVP: ✓

WEDDING GUEST LIST

NAME:	ADDRESS:	# IN PARTY:	RSVP: ✓

WEDDING GUEST LIST

NAME:	ADDRESS:	# IN PARTY:	RSVP: ✓

WEDDING GUEST LIST

NAME:	ADDRESS:	# IN PARTY:	RSVP: ✓

WEDDING GUEST LIST

NAME:	ADDRESS:	# IN PARTY:	RSVP: ✓

WEDDING GUEST LIST

NAME:	ADDRESS:	# IN PARTY:	RSVP: ✓

WEDDING GUEST LIST

NAME:	ADDRESS:	# IN PARTY:	RSVP: ✓

WEDDING GUEST LIST

NAME:	ADDRESS:	# IN PARTY:	RSVP: ✓

WEDDING GUEST LIST

NAME:	ADDRESS:	# IN PARTY:	RSVP: ✓

WEDDING GUEST LIST

NAME:	ADDRESS:	# IN PARTY:	RSVP: ✓

WEDDING GUEST LIST

NAME:	ADDRESS:	# IN PARTY:	RSVP: ✓

WEDDING GUEST LIST

NAME:	ADDRESS:	# IN PARTY:	RSVP: ✓

WEDDING GUEST LIST

NAME:	ADDRESS:	# IN PARTY:	RSVP: ✓

WEDDING GUEST LIST

NAME:	ADDRESS:	# IN PARTY:	RSVP: ✓

SEATING CHART PLANNER

TABLE #

TABLE #

TABLE #

TABLE #

SEATING PLANNER NOTES:

SEATING CHART PLANNER

TABLE #

TABLE #

TABLE #

TABLE #

SEATING PLANNER NOTES:

SEATING CHART PLANNER

TABLE #   TABLE #

TABLE #   TABLE #

SEATING PLANNER NOTES:

SEATING CHART PLANNER

TABLE #   TABLE #

TABLE #   TABLE #

SEATING PLANNER NOTES:

SEATING CHART PLANNER

TABLE #

TABLE #

TABLE #

TABLE #

SEATING PLANNER NOTES:

SEATING CHART PLANNER

TABLE #

TABLE #

TABLE #

TABLE #

SEATING PLANNER NOTES:

SEATING CHART PLANNER

TABLE #   TABLE #

TABLE #   TABLE #

SEATING PLANNER NOTES:

SEATING CHART PLANNER

TABLE #

TABLE #

TABLE #

TABLE #

SEATING PLANNER NOTES:

SEATING CHART PLANNER

TABLE #   TABLE #

TABLE #   TABLE #

SEATING PLANNER NOTES:

SEATING CHART PLANNER

TABLE #

TABLE #

TABLE #

TABLE #

SEATING PLANNER NOTES:

SEATING CHART PLANNER

TABLE #   TABLE #

TABLE #   TABLE #

SEATING PLANNER NOTES:

SEATING CHART PLANNER

TABLE #   TABLE #

TABLE #   TABLE #

SEATING PLANNER NOTES:

SEATING CHART PLANNER

TABLE #

TABLE #

TABLE #

TABLE #

SEATING PLANNER NOTES:

SEATING CHART PLANNER

TABLE #

TABLE #

TABLE #

TABLE #

SEATING PLANNER NOTES:

SEATING CHART PLANNER

TABLE #

TABLE #

TABLE #

TABLE #

SEATING PLANNER NOTES:

SEATING CHART PLANNER

TABLE #

TABLE #

TABLE #

TABLE #

SEATING PLANNER NOTES:

SEATING CHART PLANNER

TABLE #

TABLE #

TABLE #

TABLE #

SEATING PLANNER NOTES:

SEATING CHART PLANNER

TABLE #

TABLE #

TABLE #

TABLE #

SEATING PLANNER NOTES:

SEATING CHART PLANNER

TABLE #

TABLE #

TABLE #

TABLE #

SEATING PLANNER NOTES:

SEATING CHART PLANNER

TABLE #   TABLE #

TABLE #   TABLE #

SEATING PLANNER NOTES:

SEATING CHART PLANNER

TABLE #

TABLE #

TABLE #

TABLE #

SEATING PLANNER NOTES:

SEATING CHART PLANNER

TABLE #

TABLE #

TABLE #

TABLE #

SEATING PLANNER NOTES:

SEATING CHART PLANNER

TABLE #   TABLE #

TABLE #   TABLE #

SEATING PLANNER NOTES:

SEATING CHART PLANNER

TABLE #   TABLE #

TABLE #   TABLE #

SEATING PLANNER NOTES:

SEATING CHART PLANNER

TABLE #

TABLE #

TABLE #

TABLE #

SEATING PLANNER NOTES:

SEATING CHART PLANNER

TABLE #

TABLE #

TABLE #

TABLE #

SEATING PLANNER NOTES:

SEATING CHART PLANNER

TABLE #

TABLE #

TABLE #

TABLE #

SEATING PLANNER NOTES:

SEATING CHART PLANNER

TABLE #

TABLE #

TABLE #

TABLE #

SEATING PLANNER NOTES:

SEATING CHART PLANNER

TABLE #

TABLE #

TABLE #

TABLE #

SEATING PLANNER NOTES:

SEATING CHART PLANNER

TABLE #

TABLE #

TABLE #

TABLE #

SEATING PLANNER NOTES:

SEATING CHART PLANNER

TABLE #

TABLE #

TABLE #

TABLE #

SEATING PLANNER NOTES:

SEATING CHART PLANNER

TABLE #

TABLE #

TABLE #

TABLE #

SEATING PLANNER NOTES:

SEATING CHART PLANNER

TABLE #

TABLE #

TABLE #

TABLE #

SEATING PLANNER NOTES:

SEATING CHART PLANNER

TABLE #

TABLE #

TABLE #

TABLE #

SEATING PLANNER NOTES:

SEATING CHART PLANNER

TABLE #

TABLE #

TABLE #

TABLE #

SEATING PLANNER NOTES:

SEATING CHART PLANNER

TABLE #

TABLE #

TABLE #

TABLE #

SEATING PLANNER NOTES:

SEATING CHART PLANNER

TABLE #

TABLE #

TABLE #

TABLE #

SEATING PLANNER NOTES:

SEATING CHART PLANNER

TABLE #

TABLE #

TABLE #

TABLE #

SEATING PLANNER NOTES:

SEATING CHART PLANNER

TABLE #

TABLE #

TABLE #

TABLE #

SEATING PLANNER NOTES:

SEATING CHART PLANNER

TABLE #

TABLE #

TABLE #

TABLE #

SEATING PLANNER NOTES:

SEATING CHART PLANNER

TABLE #   TABLE #

TABLE #   TABLE #

SEATING PLANNER NOTES:

SEATING CHART PLANNER

TABLE #

TABLE #

TABLE #

TABLE #

SEATING PLANNER NOTES:

SEATING CHART PLANNER

TABLE #

TABLE #

TABLE #

TABLE #

SEATING PLANNER NOTES:

SEATING CHART PLANNER

TABLE #

TABLE #

TABLE #

TABLE #

SEATING PLANNER NOTES:

SEATING CHART PLANNER

TABLE #   TABLE #

TABLE #   TABLE #

SEATING PLANNER NOTES:

SEATING CHART PLANNER

TABLE #

TABLE #

TABLE #

TABLE #

SEATING PLANNER NOTES:

SEATING CHART PLANNER

TABLE #

TABLE #

TABLE #

TABLE #

SEATING PLANNER NOTES:

SEATING CHART PLANNER

TABLE #

TABLE #

TABLE #

TABLE #

SEATING PLANNER NOTES:

SEATING CHART PLANNER

TABLE #

TABLE #

TABLE #

TABLE #

SEATING PLANNER NOTES:

SEATING CHART PLANNER

TABLE #   TABLE #

TABLE #   TABLE #

SEATING PLANNER NOTES:

SEATING CHART PLANNER

TABLE #   TABLE #

TABLE #   TABLE #

SEATING PLANNER NOTES:

SEATING CHART PLANNER

TABLE #   TABLE #

TABLE #   TABLE #

SEATING PLANNER NOTES:

SEATING CHART PLANNER

TABLE #

TABLE #

TABLE #

TABLE #

SEATING PLANNER NOTES:

SEATING CHART PLANNER

TABLE #

TABLE #

TABLE #

TABLE #

SEATING PLANNER NOTES:

SEATING CHART PLANNER

TABLE #

TABLE #

TABLE #

TABLE #

SEATING PLANNER NOTES:

SEATING CHART PLANNER

TABLE #   TABLE #

TABLE #   TABLE #

SEATING PLANNER NOTES:

SEATING CHART PLANNER

TABLE #   TABLE #

TABLE #   TABLE #

SEATING PLANNER NOTES:

SEATING CHART PLANNER

TABLE #

TABLE #

TABLE #

TABLE #

SEATING PLANNER NOTES:

SEATING CHART PLANNER

TABLE #

TABLE #

TABLE #

TABLE #

SEATING PLANNER NOTES:

SEATING CHART PLANNER

TABLE #

TABLE #

TABLE #

TABLE #

SEATING PLANNER NOTES:

SEATING CHART PLANNER

TABLE #

TABLE #

TABLE #

TABLE #

SEATING PLANNER NOTES:

Made in the USA
Middletown, DE
31 August 2023

37622907R00086